Chardi-kla

"A Proven Success Secret"

Chardi-kla

"A Proven Success Secret"

An exclusive group of people have been using this success secret, for more than 500 years, and are achieving the ultimate success.

Author: PJ Bath

Dedication

I dedicate this book to my parents, wife and two sons; Sahil and Jaipal, who are my inspiration in everything I do. I love you all.

"Avval Allah Noor Upaya Qudrat Keh Sub Banday;
Aik Noor Keh Sub Jag Upajiya Kaun Bhale Ko Mandhe"

Guru Granth Sahib

Translation
"God Created Light, Of Which All The Beings Were Born;
From The Light, The Universe. So Who Is Good And Who Is Bad"

A Special Note for Readers

This book is written at the average 6th grade (12 years old) student's understanding level. Simple sentence structure and basic vocabulary have been used throughout the book. Some readers might find this book's English to be below their competency level. However, every reader will be able to benefit from the ideas presented in this book.

Contents

"The key to growth is the introduction of higher dimensions of consciousness into our awareness"
Lao Tzu

Introduction

The world has been in an economic downturn for few years now. Many organizations and families have gone bankrupt. Millions of people are under enormous stress and are struggling to meet their obligations.

Most people are living in fear every day. Either it's fear of losing their job, fear of losing their house, fear of not meeting all their obligations, fear of disease, fear of death, etc. It is very unfortunate that in these abundant times, we are still facing all these fears.

Human beings have made a lot of progress in the last 100 years. We are richer than previous societies, but many people are still struggling with their lives.

We all want to become successful in our lives, so we can eliminate or reduce these fears. Most of us want to live in nicer homes, drive expensive cars, travel around the world, have money for our children's education and have money for retirement.

In this book, I will share a proven formula of success, which will give you all the above.

A specific group of people have been using this formula for more than 500 years, and they have been achieving enormous success.

There are many success techniques available now, but I haven't found one, with hundreds of years of a track record, before I found this success secret.

If you are willing to learn and practice their simple success formula, this book is for you. I promise, if you practice this fine tuned and proven formula, you will definitely become successful.

This is a golden key of success. You will become a prosperous, happier and healthier person.

"Some people dream of success, while others wake up and work hard at it."

Anonymous

Prologue

It was around 5:00 PM and an Air Canada plane was about to land at the Pearson International Airport in Toronto, Canada. This flight was coming from London (UK), and about 320 people were on board. There were some newcomers onboard, who were coming to Canada for the first time.

Samuel Tushar was on this flight with his wife, and two young kids. This was to be their first time in Canada. His son and daughter were 9 and11 years old at the time, and he and his wife were around 35 years old. He was very excited, because he has always dreamt about living in Canada and finally this dream was about to come true.

During the flight, he met Jasvir Singh, who was sitting next to him. Jasvir was also coming to Canada for the first time. They spoke for hours about their past, future plans and other stuff.

They formed a friendship with each other on the flight. They exchanged their contact information and promised to stay in touch.

The flight landed safely in Toronto. Samuel and his family went through the immigration process, and they got the final stamps of permanent residency.

Samuel was a bank manager in his country, and his wife was a school teacher. They knew that they won't get the same jobs in Canada upon their arrival. They were aware that they would have to improve their English speaking skills, and then should be able to get into their professions.

So, Samuel started to look for a clerical job. He faxed his resume to many organizations over the next month, but no one gave him a job. Finally, he applied for a laborer job in a factory and was offered the job.

He reported on the job 7:00 AM Monday morning. A shift supervisor welcomed him and introduced him to the staff. He gave him the factory tour and showed him the type of work done by the company.

Samuel's first assignment was to sweep the factory floor. Samuel could not believe that he was asked to sweep the floor.

His heart fell to the floor. He felt like telling some things to the supervisor, but somehow he controlled his emotions.

This was the worst thing, which has happened to him. He was a bank manager of a major bank. He had a very nice office, a servant and a secretary to assist him plus a staff of about 20 people. He even had a servant at home to help his wife.

He thought about all his responsibilities. He had to be a man and do whatever it takes to feed his family.

So, he grabbed the broom and started sweeping the floor. This was the lowest moment in his life. He had big plans for the future, but for a moment he thought that they were not realistic.

He swept the floor for the rest of the day, and headed home at the end of his shift.

He came home around 5:30 PM, and narrated the first day's episode to his wife. After hearing the story, she started crying. She could not believe what she heard. They were living a good life in their country, but came to Canada for a better life.

They realized that, this is a new start for them. They hoped that everything would be fine in few years.

By the time Samuel had been working at the factory for six months, he was still earning minimum wage and was struggling to make ends meet. His kids were in school, and wife was working at a restaurant. They were going through a lot of up and downs.

He was taking English courses, and became somewhat fluent. He had an evaluation done on his education and was ready to enter his true profession. He applied for a management job at a few banks, but he had no luck.

He called Jasvir Singh (the man who he met on the plane) to find out, how he was doing. Jasvir was a lawyer in his country. He told Samuel that he was also struggling to adjust in the new country, but financially he was doing ok; he was working 15-16 hours every day, though.

Samuel was surprised to hear that Jasvir was working that many hours. Jasvir told him that if he wants to succeed, he will have to give up time now to have time with his family in the future. Jasvir offered that he would like to help Samuel, and suggested that they should meet.

Samuel thanked him, and said that he will call him back to schedule the time for a meeting. He also told Jasvir that he can just call him Sam.

A year has gone by, and Sam was still struggling. He finally decided to contact Jasvir and ask for help.

Jasvir was opening a grocery store. He offered Sam the store manager job. Sam gladly accepted the job, but he was astounded by the success of Jasvir. They came to Canada on the same day, and he is still struggling, whereas Jasvir was doing very well.

He started to work at Jasvir's store. However, he was very curious about Jasvir's success. So, he asked Jasvir, what was the secret of his success?

Hard work, Jasvir replied.

Don't be funny, Sam said. I have been working hard too. There are lots of people in the world, who work hard, but struggle to meet necessities of life.

Again, Sam pleaded Jasvir to share the secret of his success.

Finally, Jasvir told Sam that secret of his success is "Chardi-kla". Jasvir said that it is a golden key to prosperous, happy and healthy life.

He said that this formula has been in practice for more than 500 years, and people have been achieving unmatched success.

He asked Sam to do his own research on "Chardi-kla", if he really wants to understand the formula.

So, Sam decided to research Jasvir's success formula – "Chardi-kla"

"If you itch for success, keep on scratching."

Anonymous

1

Success Research

Sam spent the next two years, trying to figure out the success formula. He read dozens of books about success, and achievements.

He also started practicing the success techniques, which he learned from the books. He had some successes, but it has not been consistent.

In the meantime, Jasvir has opened a few more businesses. He was very pleasant and flamboyant. They become good friends, and Jasvir always encourages Sam to be happy and stay in "Chardi-kla".

Even though, Sam still doesn't quite understand what "Chardi-kla" is, however, Jasvir's contagious personality influences Sam.

So far, Sam has found this about success:

Success

Success is a magical word. When someone talks about success, we generally start thinking about being rich and famous. Pictures of nice homes and cars run through our minds. For a moment, a feeling of happiness and peace runs through our bodies.

Most of us don't consider ourselves successful, until we have enough money. But, what is enough money?

We all have a different definition of enough money. So, we all keep going after the success without knowing, what success is and what does it mean to us?

The whole world is striving for success as Countries, communities and individuals. Some of the people have reached a state of success, but most are still searching.

The meaning of success comes in many forms. It depends on what you are searching for in your life.

An athlete may have one definition of success, and a stay at home Mom may have another. A musician may see success as a number one hit, and a doctor may see success as a surgery, that went well.

It all really depends on the perspective of life, that you have. Perspectives of success are as numerous as people on this planet or stars in the sky.

However, if we narrow down the success in few main forms, it would be:

1. Earning enough money to meet all your obligations.
2. Healthy life.
3. Happier Life.

Most of us believe that when we achieve everything, we desire; we will be successful. We keep acquiring material things to have a moment of happiness and a peace of mind.

Success is not a place to be. It is a journey. Success is a practice of certain behaviors. If we practice these success behaviors, we will achieve everything we desire.

Most of the success books that Sam read, suggested that first a person should decide, what success means to him or her.

Write down your definition of success on a piece paper. Read your written definition few times and observe if it is in tune with your personality and true self.

Success Resources

There are thousands of books available about success. There are also thousands of success coaches, who have developed success techniques. These coaches are trying their best to help people to achieve higher levels of success.

Sam admires all the coaches, who have chosen this field and are helping people realize their potential, but he feels that some techniques are very difficult to follow. People need simple success techniques to get on the road of success.

Our school systems prepare us for jobs and other challenges in life. However, schools don't teach us how to be successful. We all learn by making mistakes, and continue to do so.

By the time, we learn and prepare for success; we have spent 50+ years. People start thinking about retirement at this age. At this point, there is usually little motivation to pursue success.

So far, Sam hadn't found any information about "Chardi-kla". He was frustrated, that this is such a big secret!

Finally, Sam asked Jasvir to provide assistance in figuring out "Chardi-kla". Jasvir told Sam, that he won't find anything about this formula in books. He suggested that he should look at operating behavior of specific communities, and the answer will be obvious.

Behavior Research

Sam wanted to find easy and consistent success techniques. He knew that even though, we live in a small world, we still have close knit communities. People tend to associate with people who speak their mother tongue and practice the same faith.

He started looking at different communities and their living styles. Then suddenly, he decided to research the community to which Jasvir belonged.

He noticed that this specific group of people is enjoying unmatched success and happiness in this competitive and stressful world. He asked Jasvir, if he was on the right track, and Jasvir confirmed it.

He spent the next year investigating, what "Chardi-kla" is made of, and how it is practiced.

He found that these people have faced the most adversity in modern human history, but they are going very strong. They had to fight for their survival, because the rulers of different times wanted to eliminate these people from the face of the planet.

Sam told this to his wife, and she asked a question:

"Why did the rulers of the time wanted to eliminate these people from the planet?"

"Because they fought injustice, and protected the underdogs." Sam replied.

He said that these people are fearless and courageous. They are action oriented and failure is not a part of their existence.

They have this simple success formula, which has made them a very powerful force in the world. Their formula is so much engraved in them, that most of them don't even realize, that they are using this method of success.

During his research, Sam also collected tangible facts about the success of the formula, and people who have been using this formula. He reviewed his findings with his boss and friend Jasvir, and got his stamp of approval on the formula.

By this time Jasvir had multiple businesses. Sam's wife also started to work in Jasvir's business. Sam was happy with his progress. He achieved enough financial stability that he was able to purchase a house.

He realized that due to his association with Jasvir, he had been practicing "Chardikla" unknowingly to a certain level. His personality changed and life was becoming better day by day.

Sam also had enrolled in a "Mind Controlling Techniques" course, which was being held over a few weekends at a local college.

"Education is what remains after one has forgotten everything that he learned in school."

Albert Einstein

2

Class One

One Saturday morning, Sam was attending the "Mind Controlling Techniques" course. There were about 30 people in the class, it was a diverse group.

The instructor was 62 year old Luis, and she had been teaching for 33 years. Course started with the introductions and some information about the participants' professions. Luis had requested everyone to provide a reason, why are they attending this course and what would they like to get out of the course?

After the introductions, it was apparent that everyone was taking the course to learn how to control their minds in order to attract:

- Prosperity.
- Happiness.
- Good Health.
- Success.

Some discussion about the behavior of successful people occurred in the class. Everyone said that they want to be millionaires, and travel around the world.

Luis mentioned that most millionaires work, more than 60 hours per week. Furthermore, they are also avid readers. They are so curious that they continuously learn. They understand that reading is to the mind, as the exercise is to the body. They give up the non-value added activities in their life.

People wondered; why would the millionaires be working so hard? They already have enough money.

Luis said that millionaires don't work for money, they are just so driven to contribute to the society that money becomes secondary. Remember though, there are not too many millionaires in the world. They are the minority in the world.

One of the participants, Cynthia, said that most of the people in the world struggle through life. She heard that about 50% of the people go to bed every night, without food. She said that we are very lucky to live in this country.

Luis agreed with Cynthia's statement. Even though, we live in one of the prosperous countries, we still have lots of people, who are living unhappy lives. That's why this "Mind Controlling Techniques" course was developed.

As Earl Nightingale said years ago: "We become what we think about; most of the time".

Studies have proven again and again, that we are the product of our own thoughts. Our outer life is a reflection of our inner life.

If you learn the techniques that we teach you in this course, you will definitely have tools to change your life. You will be able to change your inner life by controlling your thoughts, and that will change your outer life.

Sam raised his hand up indicating that he wanted to say something.

Luis stopped, and asked Sam if he has a question?

Sam said that he has done lots of research in the last few years on success. And, he told his and Jasvir's story to the class.

"I don't know, what these Punjabi guys are doing, but they become very successful, wherever they go" said Cynthia "I'm jealous of their success."

"They have a unique success secret" Sam replied.

"What! Success secret?!" Cynthia shouted.

"Yes" Sam answered proudly. It took me three years to figure out their success formula. Plus, I wanted to make sure that it is not a fluke, so I have done extensive research on their success formula. And, let me tell you guys, I have never seen any success technique work so consistently. These guys have been using this success formula for more than 500 years, and are having tremendous success.

"I guess, we should learn that success secret, instead of learning these mind controlling techniques" Stacy suggested.

"Hold on, people. I think we are getting off track here. We should get back into our course material" said Luis.

"No, we are serious" Cynthia said. "We need to learn something, which has a proven track record, and can be easily used. If these Punjabi folks have been using this formula for more than 500 hundred years, it must be working."

Everyone convinced Luis that she should let Sam share his research and formula with everyone in the class.

Luis agreed to let Sam share the formula in the class, but she wanted to go over her material first. Everyone agreed to go through the course material first. They requested Sam to present the "Success Formula" in the last class.

Sam agreed that he will share all his research with the class, but he needs at least four hours to do it.

"Let's get going guys" said Luis. "I am curious to learn about this formula too. Sam, we will give you the full afternoon of the last day of our course."

"I'll be ready" Sam answered.

"Being ignorant is not so shameful as being unwilling to learn."

Anonymous

3

Last Class

It was the last day of the course, and everyone was looking forward to learning the secret success formula from Sam.

"We have covered most of the course, material" said Luis. "We have done well with our time. I have about an hour's material to go over."

"Hopefully, Sam is ready" said Cynthia.

"I'm ready" Sam replied.

Luis said that she would like to cover the last chapter of the "Mind controlling techniques" manual. Then, she would like to review the course material quickly. And, at the end, she will have the assessment quiz. Everyone agreed with Luis.

For the next three hours, Luis covered and reviewed the required material. She had the class complete the assessment quiz.

"Well done everyone" said Luis. "We have completed the course as planned, and now we can have Sam share his research and success formula with us, but if someone wants to leave, they can."

"I guess I'm going to leave then" said Richard.

"You don't want to learn the success secret of the Punjabi people?" asked Luis.

"No, I don't need to learn about anyone's secret. I am already sick of them coming over and taking our jobs!" replied Richard and walked out.

"Some people are not big enough to learn from others" said Bob, who has been sitting quietly in the back.

Luis said that she will like to share some rules of good living with everyone, before Sam starts:

1. Be open to learning from every person, you come in contact with. So, keep your mind open.

2. Stay away from people, who tell you that they know everything. There is no person on this universe, who knows everything about everything. These people don't know, that they don't know, what they don't know. There is a technical term for those people "The go nowhere crowd".

(Everyone laughed when Luis said, "The go no where crowd".)

3. Be like a sponge. Absorb everything you observe. Be a student of life.

4. Strive to become the person, who people would like to associate with.

5. Do not criticize others, because you would do the same if you were in their shoes.

Now, I request Sam to share his research and the secret success formula, which we have been talking about for last four days.

"If it is a Miracle, any sort of evidence will answer, but if is a Fact, proof is necessary."
Mark Twain

4

The Proof

Sam starts: "Good afternoon, everyone."

"After some thinking about how I can effectively share my research with everyone in this class, I prepared a presentation to describe the Punjabi's secret success formula. I will try not to put you to sleep, though."

"First, I will share some history and proof about the success of this formula. We live in a world, where data rules. I have heard people say 'We believe in God, but everyone else should provide data.' Is there anyone in here, who just believes what they hear? Can I have a show of hands?"

"None? Good. I didn't think there would be anyone here, who blindly believes what they hear. I already shared my story with the class last week. I have been associating with Jasvir and his friends for about four years now.

These Punjabi people are very energetic, flamboyant and happy. They have a very positive outlook on life. They have a very rich history and culture, which has not yet been thoroughly studied.

Has anyone done any research on their history?"

"I know a little bit about their culture." said Bob. "I know about their music, and I have seen the Bhangra dance. I know that Punjabi music is very popular in the world today."

Stacy said that all she knows about them is that they live in all major countries in the world. They are one of the hard working communities in this country and in the world. They are the Sikh Faith People from Punjab, India.

"So, some of you know a bit about the Punjabi people. All of the Punjabi people are not from Punjab. They also live in other parts of India, and yes, they live in almost every country in the world."

"What is the difference between a Sikh and a Punjabi?" asked Luis.

"Sikh is a specific way of life. It is a faith and the people who believe in it follow the teachings of Guru Granth Sahib. Punjab is a state in India, and about 60% of the people who live there, are Sikhs, other 40% are Hindu, Muslim, Christian, and people who follow other faiths. People who speak the Punjabi language are called Punjabi's, and they may be from any faith.

Most of the people you see as successful are Punjabi Sikhs, and we will discuss their success secret. I don't want you feel that I am preaching the Sikh faith. I am not preaching any faith at all.

I have been practicing their success formula for a while, and my life has improved in every way. I just want to share my research with the class, which is based on the Sikh people success. So just keep an open mind and try to understand the formula.

If you can grasp, and practice this formula, I promise you, that you will get whatever you desire in your life. These people have been practicing this formula for more than 500 years, and it is error proof.

Before I move on, let me share some contributions (facts), that these people have made using this formula:

Facts

- Punjab produces about 20 percent of India's wheat, with only 1.5 percent of land.
- Punjab produces about 12 percent of India's rice, with 1.5 percent of land.

- Punjab is one of the richest and happiest states in India.
- Of the persons executed during the freedom struggle with the British in India 60 percent were Sikhs (Punjabi's).
- 60 percent of the Indian Liberation Army Officers during the British rule were Sikhs (Punjabi's).
- 20 percent of the British Indian Army during World War one were Sikhs (Punjabi's).
- 73 percent of the people killed in atrocities by the British were Sikhs (Punjabi's).
- 80 percent of the people sent to the gallows by the British were Sikhs (Punjabi's).
- 61 percent of the people killed by the British Army at Jallianwalla Bagh were Sikhs (Punjabi's).

If you look at these facts: only 2% of the people are contributing around 60% in most areas. How is that possible?

I will explain with a very brief history of these people, so you can understand that they have been using this formula for years.

History

"The Sikh faith was established in the early 15th century in Punjab, India. Most of the people; who joined this faith were farmers (because Punjab is a farming state), or worked in other physical labor related fields.

For the first 300 years of their existence, they had to fight for their survival. Every ruler has tried to eliminate these people from the planet; however with the guidance of their teachers, they persevered and become victorious."

"Why did the rulers of the time wanted to eliminate these people from the planet?" asked Cynthia.

"My wife asked me the same question, when I told her about this" replied Sam. "And the answer is that they confronted injustice, and protected the underdogs."

"My research shows that the Mughal Empire was kicked out of India, by these people.

If you notice that, it is only been little over 500 years, since their inception. If for the first 300 years they fought for their survival, then actually, it's only been 200 years (approximately) of a growth period that they have had. Even in these last 200 years, they faced many adverse events.

In 1799 they established their own kingdom (The Sikh Empire) in Punjab and ruled for about 50 years."

"What happened after 50 years" asked Luis.

"The British Empire took over their empire" answered Sam.

Status Today

"In this short period of time, Punjabi people have become a major economic force in the world. They are living in almost every country in the world.

They own small and big businesses. They hold senior level positions in some major companies; however, their niche market is small businesses.

My research shows that they are one of the happiest communities in the world. They consist of approximately 26 million people located around the world. As I already mentioned, about 60% of them live in Punjab, India. They have very pleasant personalities and are action oriented ("The go getters").

What I noticed is that they are known for a grand style of living. Whatever they do; they do it in style. They live in nice homes, drive nice cars, pay for their children's education, and live according to their faith. The bottom line is that, they are living prosperous and happy lives."

"How are they doing it?" Cynthia asked.

"Isn't it unbelievable, that they are living prosperous and happy lives in this hectic world?" Sam asked. "Also, how can a small community, in this big world, become so successful in this short period of time?"

"That's what we need to know!" said Cynthia. "How can a small group of farmers and their support workers become so successful?"

"Does anyone think that it is some kind of magic...?" Sam asked again. "No, there is no magic. They know and practice something that other people around the world don't. I didn't know this until I came in contact with Jasvir. Let me tell you, it is not just this positive thinking that we hear about these days. There is a lot more than that!"

"Please tell us the formula!" said Cynthia. "I am dying to learn this formula."

"The formula is called Chardi-kla" said Sam.

"Huh... what does that mean?" asked Cynthia.

Sam answered that this formula has many components, and that he will explain that later. First, he said, that he needs to share the adversity that these people have been through. Once you see the adversity, you will understand that this formula really works.

"While you are alive, conquer death, and you shall have no regrets in the end."

Guru Granth Sahib

5

Adversity

"Now let me share some information about the adversity that they went through. As I already said, every ruler in India during the years 1500-1800 has tried to wipe these people out from the face of the earth.

I understand that often rulers are very insecure. They just want people to do what they are told to do, but the Sikhs stood up against injustice and protected weak people.

As you know, a picture is worth thousand words. Now, I will show you some slides, which will shake your mind and body. These slides show the adversity that they experienced. And, adversity is the root of this formula."

Bhai Mani Singh Martyrdom

During the Mughal Empire, no Sikh was allowed to say the word "Guru". The Mughals had put a price on the head of every Sikh. Bhai Mani Singh refused to give up his beliefs, and in 1733, he was cut up into pieces joint by joint.

"The Power of Chardi-kla"

Bhai Mati Das Martyrdom

The Mughal rulers tried to intimidate the Ninth Guru by torturing and killing Sikhs. Bhai Mati Das was also asked to give up his faith, which he refused, and he was cut with a saw from his head downwards in front of the Guru in 1675.

"The Power of Chardi-kla"

Bhai Dayala Martyrdom

Bhai Dayala Ji was also asked to give up his Faith, which he refused. He was boiled in a cauldron of water in 1675.

"The Power of Chardi-kla"

Bhai Taru Singh Martyrdom

Bhai Taru Singh was given the choice
between giving up his belief and death. He
was asked to cut of his hair and present to
the ruler. He refused and his scalp was cut
away with razors to prevent his hair ever
growing back (in 1745).

"The Power of Chardi-kla"

Infant Children Martyrdom

During the 1750's, Mughal Empire Governer Mir Mannu, took the responsibility to finish the Sikhs. Children were cut into pieces. Garlands of the children body parts were put around their mother's necks.

"The Power of Chardi-kla"

Infant Children Martyrdom

During the 1750's, Mughal Empire Governer Mir Mannu, took the responsibility to finish the Sikhs. Infant children were transfixed with spears in front of their mothers.

"The Power of Chardi-kla"

The Tenth Guru's Young Sons Martyrdom

These two brave young souls (aged 5 and 7 years), were bricked alive by the soldiers of the Mughal Empire, because they refused to give up their beliefs (in 1705).

"The Power of Chardi-kla"

A Few Adversities without Pictures

Guru Tegh Bahadur Martyrdom

Guru Tegh Bahadur committed to protect the Hindu Pundits, who were being forced to give up their faith. The Guru made a decision to risk his life in order to protect the right of the Hindus to practice their faith freely. This Guru set an example for all Sikh's to protect the rights of people of all the faiths.

Jallianwala Bagh Massacre

In 1919, British Indian Army killed hundreds of innocent people (majority of whom were Sikh's) during one of the largest Sikh religious festivals – the Vaisakhi.

"The Power of Chardi-kla"

1984 Killings of Sikh's

More than 3000 unarmed Sikh men, women and children were burnt alive in New Delhi in 1984. No justice has ever been served for these killings since 1984.

Note:

These are only few pictures and facts. These people have faced thousands of situations, like these, since their inception.

"The Power of Chardi-kla"

"Has any of you ever seen these pictures before?" asked Sam.

"No!" said the participants.

"I am somewhat surprised, but on the other hand, as I already said, their vast history and culture have not been commonly studied."

"Did all that really happen?" asked Luis.

"According to my research, it definitely happened" answered Sam. But you might want to do your own research if you are interested.

To be frank with you, the first time I saw these pictures, I was depressed for few days. Then I realized that all this adversity has made them stronger. They are reaching new heights in the Global community, even though they have been through all this.

"Let me be clear once again here. I am not talking about or promoting Sikh faith" said Sam. "I just want to share the research I have done on their success.

Please let me know, if you are not comfortable, and I will stop here."

"Please keep going. We all are grown up, and we live in the Global community. We need to learn from each other" said Bob.

Luis said: "We are all one God's children anyway. We should learn from anyone we can. If their success formula can help others, we should learn it and use it."

"I definitely want to learn this formula. Plus you are not asking us to practice the Sikh faith, and you are not even Sikh yourself." said Bob.

"Yes, I am not a Sikh, and this formula does not require anyone to practice the Sikh faith" said Sam.

"If we can use this formula and improve our lives, we will use it." said Cynthia, "If not, then we won't use it. It's that simple."

"I agree. It is just an education session." said Luis. "We learn new things every day, some people use what they learn and some don't, so, please keep on going.

Sam replied "Ok". Now I will explain the formula in detail."

"Have firm faith, and let your mind be not shaken."

Guru Granth Sahib

6

Faith

The Foundation of Chardi-kla

As I said earlier, name of the formula is 'Chardi-kla' and it means "the rising power of the mind". It is pronounced as:

Ch   as in <u>ch</u>apter

Ar   as in <u>are</u>

Di   as in <u>Dee</u>

Kla   as in <u>Kla</u>us

There are five elements to 'Chardi-kla' and before I fully discuss this tremendous power of the mind, I will discuss all five elements in detail.

    First, I will discuss the foundation, which is **faith**. When I say faith, I am not talking about any specific religious faith; I am talking about faith in the infinite power. Faith in one God and that is, the Universal God.

Sam grabbed a marker and drew a rectangle on the board, and wrote the word faith in it.

FAITH

"By the way, just for our information, what do they call God? I mean by what name?" asked Cynthia.

"They call God by the name of "Waheguru", and that means "The Wonderful Guru" answered Sam. However, here I'm not talking about faith in the name. It is faith in the Universal God, and we all have different names for God.

"So, getting back to our success formula...The people who practice Chardi-kla; their faith is very, very strong. They don't believe that they do anything themselves."

"What! They don't believe in themselves?!!" Cynthia shouted.

"No, they definitely believe in themselves, but they just don't take any credit themselves." replied Sam. "When they succeed, they give all the credit to God."

"Who gets the cursing, when they fail?" Cynthia asked again.

Sam answered that they take the blame themselves. They analyze the situation, and figure out, what they did wrong. They don't give up though, because they understand that the accumulated effort will pay off.

A strong faith is the motivating force in the lives of the people who use this formula. Strong faith helps them get through all the adversities of life (as shown on the examples before).

"Psychological studies show that people who have faith in the Universal Power (or One God) are happier in their lives. They are more driven to contribute to the society, and go the extra mile to serve their fellow human beings.

Strong faith also increases our ability to bounce back from unpleasant events. I understand, that the day to day responsibilities and problems put so much pressure on us, that sometimes we tend to question our faith.

All the research I have done on success, over the last few years, suggests that faith is the main component of success. Interesting part of my research is that these Punjabi people have been practicing this for more than 500 years, and succeeding, whereas these psychological studies were done in the last 50-60 years.

We all know that everyday life problems put an emotional strain on people. Common stressors of everyday life form negative energy, and faith helps us cope with that negative energy. Remember that faith provides emotional support, and that support is always there; it is up to us to use it.

This is where these Punjabi people are excelling. What I found is that whatever they do, they start with the name of God and end with the same.

Their faith is so strong in the Infinite Power that, they believe that it is in them. They believe that the only thing that is in their control is their **effort**.

They do not worry about the outcome.

They live with constant reminders of their faith, and **they expect the best**.

They also cultivate the attitude of acceptance, and accept failure or unpleasant situations while trying to do their best. They don't curl up; instead they rise to the challenge.

"Most people try to do their best in any situation" said Cynthia.

"I'm not sure Cynthia. I have seen lots of people blame others for their circumstances. Better yet, I was one of those people, before I came in contact with Jasvir. I have even seen people blame their luck or God. Jasvir told me that when we blame others, we show a weakness in our faith. We feel the faith as a burden, and not a guide, and that is the seed of failure.

What I found is, that these people are trained from childhood that faith in one God is the most important thing in life, and they consistently remind themselves of this throughout each day.

So, whatever religion you practice, have an unconditional faith in God.

Faith will help you keep your optimism intact. It will keep you going in the direction you want to go. Faith will cure indecisiveness and will give you the confidence to make decisions. If you make faith the driving force in your life, as the Punjabi people have done, you will feel very close to the Universal Power and believe that God is there to help. Faith provides inner strength, and that is why this is the foundation of the success formula – Chardi-kla.

I know, that you all wanted to know, how Punjabi people achieve above average success in a short period of time. That was my question too, before I did my research. All the adversity they went through made them stronger. Their faith is so strong that it helped their predecessors get through all those problems.

They train their children to learn from adversity and not to dwell on problems. Faith is part of their DNA, and they believe that God will help anyone who will reach out to the Universal Power. They believe that faith is the boat that carries us across the river of life. Faith is the foundation of Chardi-kla.

There are four pillars of Chardikla, and I will explain those one by one as well. Let's move on to pillar number one...

"Your work is to discover your work, and then with all your heart to give yourself to it."

Buddha

7

Diligent Work
Pillar One

First pillar of Chardi-kla is working diligently. Most of you already know how hard Punjabi people work. It doesn't matter what type of work it is. They will take the job and get it done.

Sam drew the following on the board.

```
┌─────┐
│  D  │
│  I  │
│  L  │
│  L  │
│  I  │
│  G  │
│  E  │
│  N  │
│  T  │
│     │
│  W  │
│  O  │
│  R  │
│  K  │
└─────┴──────────────────────────────┐
│            FAITH                    │
│          (Foundation)               │
└─────────────────────────────────────┘
```

What I found with my association with them is that most Punjabi people work very hard, whether it is working for someone else or for themselves. They don't consider any type of work to be bad.

They are trained from childhood to put their heart and soul into their work. Most of them work at least 60 hours per week.

"WOW! Why do they work so many hours? Most people struggle to work 40 hours per week." said Cynthia.

"Because they are trained to work hard and try to contribute their best" Sam replied. "Work is a passion for the Punjabi people, and they make a good living by working extra hard. During my research, I found that on average, most millionaires work 60 or more hours per week."

"What? Are they nuts?!!" Cynthia exclaimed again.

Everyone had a loud laugh at this.

"Believe it or not, this is actually true" said Sam. "What I found is that these successful Punjabi people believe from the core, that they have to do their part first, and then God will do his part. It's like planting the seed first, and then God will nurture the plant. Another thing I noticed during my research is that hard workers are also respected in the Punjabi community. People who don't work for living are not regarded high in the community."

"If you do some research, you will not find many Punjabi people on social assistance programs."

"They don't take any government assistance programs?" asked Luis.

"They do, but only what they perceive to be legitimate assistance" Sam replied. They will accept EI benefits, pension benefits & medical benefits, because we all contribute into those programs.

These people believe that food stamps, residential assistance, and similar programs are for unfortunate people, who are unable to earn a good living, and Punjabi people don't consider themselves unfortunate, instead they consider themselves fortunate.

"Wow! What an attitude to have!" said Luis.

"After all they have been through, they still consider themselves fortunate?" asked Cynthia.

"That's the magic of 'Chardi-kla'. Honest earning is their first responsibility, and they do a very good job on that."

You may have noticed that most Punjabi people are self employed or run small businesses. They have an entrepreneurial mindset, and they try to get into business as soon as possible.

Here are a few reasons for that:

- They prefer to be their own bosses.
- They can work as many hours as they want it, if it is their own business.

- They understand the potential to expand their business.
- They can serve many people with their business.

This pillar of 'Chardi-kla' holds the power to contribute to the society and to your maximum ability. The Universal Power is constantly seeking to be a great service to mankind, and it seeks a channel whereby it can create the greatest benefit."

"So, these people think that the Universal Power is trying to serve mankind through them?" asked Cynthia.

"No, they understand that the Universal Power seeks to serve mankind through the people who participate in the greatest activity. They just participate diligently and try to do their best to serve mankind."

As we all know, idle thinking will not get you any results. Thinking needs to be supported with activity, and that's what successful people do.

"But shouldn't we have a plan before we get involved into activity?" asked Cynthia.

"I totally agree that we must have a plan before we act on something," replied Sam. But lots of people in the world make plans and don't take any action. They don't follow through on their own plans. It is like the people who make New Year's resolutions; studies show that only 8% of these people keep their resolutions.

My research shows that if we make a habit of working diligently, we will definitely succeed. As Thomas J. Watson said: "If you want to succeed double your failure rate." So keep yourself in action; that is what Punjabi people do.

Make a decision to work diligently on whatever you take on. Put your heart and soul into your work, and you will have the first pillar of 'Chardi-kla' on your side.

"Courage is knowing, what not to fear."

Plato

8

Courage
Pillar Two

"Let's talk about the second pillar of Chardi-kla, which is Courage. These people believe that they are 'born from the sword'. They are fearless risk takers. They are trained to protect the underdogs."

Sam drew another pillar on the board.

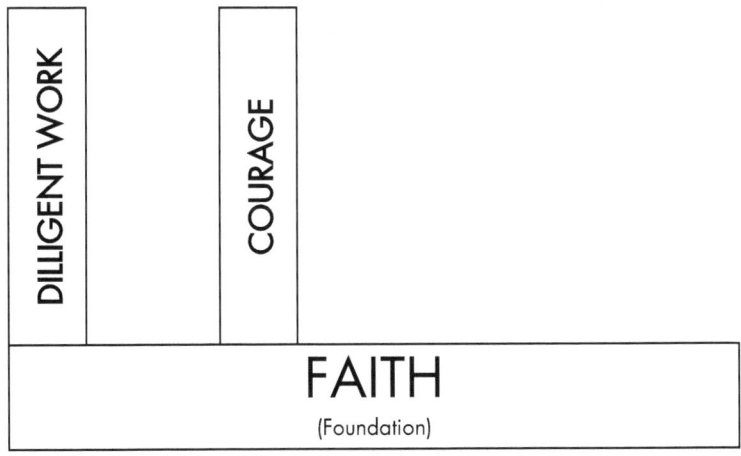

"What does 'born from the sword' mean?" asked Bob.

"What I found out is that in 1699, their 10th Guru (Guru Gobind Singh) established the initiation ceremony. It is a Sikh baptism ceremony where baptismal water (they call it Amrit) was given to the people. Baptismal water was prepared with a double edged sword, and it is considered a rebirth for a Sikh.

If you want to learn more about this religious practice, I encourage you to do more research on your own." answered Sam. "This is why they believe that they are 'born from the sword' and this is still a common practice today. It is a fascinating story. During this ceremony, the name Singh was given to all of the men of this faith and the name Kaur was given to all the women."

"What do those names mean?" asked Cynthia.

"Singh means Lion, and Kaur means Princess and every Sikh person has these names as part of their full name.

"I guess if someone believes that he or she is born from a sword, they would obviously be more courageous" said Cynthia.

"On top of that, they call themselves lions!" said Luis

"They don't just believe it. They practice courage in every moment." said Sam. As we all know, that Lion's heart is considered to be the bravest.

"Most of us have many kinds of fears, and these fears limit our potential. To overcome our fears, we need to practice gut level courage. When we practice courage, we activate our internal force, which transforms our courage into self confidence."

"But I don't believe that it is possible to be fearless." said Cynthia.

"Why not?" asked Sam.

"Well, we have so many insecurities in life, and our job is one of them. We have to feed our families, cover expenses, worry about health, etc." said Cynthia.

People, who practice 'Chardi-kla', do not worry about these things though." said Sam. Their faith is so strong that they are certain that God is going to take care of all the necessities of life. As I already said: they believe, that they just have to their part. And yes, it may not be possible for most people to be fearless, but we can definitely manage our fears.

Let's look at fear itself:

FEAR = False Experiences Appearing Real.

Most of our fears never become real. During my research, I read that 91% of our fears never materialize.

"I guess it is true that if we have nothing to fear, we cannot be conquered." said Bob.

"These people believe that becoming courageous and fearless is a matter of being honest and faithful to the creator. Fear is a feeling of inadequacy, and God doesn't make inadequate people. He does not make any junk. People who practice Chardi-kla feel that they are the best creation of God and should act accordingly.

I know that it is not easy for people to be courageous all the time; however, we should at least try to act courageous. We can experience fearlessness by taking our minds off our fears."

"It is easier said, than done." said Cynthia.

"I guess you have to give up your doubts to feel courageous." answered Sam.

"I understand, but how come these people can conquer their fears so easily?" asked Cynthia.

"As I said earlier, they believe that they are born from the sword, and being courageous and fearless is part of their DNA." replied Sam. They have been practicing courage and fearlessness for more than 500 years, and have mastered it.

Being courageous and fearless is a habit, and it becomes easier with practice.

It's easier to follow habitual patterns. When we start practicing courage, it develops our core strength, which is very powerful.

If you practice being courageous, you will create uplifting living situations. Nobody will be able to challenge your reality.

When we live courageous lives, we expect good things to happen. **And, whatever we expect usually happens according to the 'Law of Expectations.'**

In my research, I found that these Punjabi people never see anything as a problem, and their minds are not filled with past or future consequences.

Being a courageous means extending yourself beyond the limited viewpoint.

They feel that they can do anything. This is the attitude they have developed. Their motive is to be courageous, and do what's right, right now, instead of anything theoretical.

With courage, they live joyful lives. They always have a sense of celebration, and regular ups and downs of life don't bother them. I have been practicing 'Chardi-kla' myself for a while, and I have become very courageous in the process.

With my association with Jasvir, I learned that we can always find reasons to be afraid, but he taught me to ignore my fears.

He said never pay attention to fears, because God is with you, and He will destroy your fears, before they reach you. Jasvir always says that the super power is with you, and not to be afraid.

I suggest that you could also trust that the super power is with you. When you start practicing courage, you will start to feel victorious.

Courage is the second pillar of this success formula. Now, I will move to the third pillar.

"We should take a break" said Luis.

Everyone agreed and class took 15 minutes break.

"Give, and it shall be given to you. For whatever measure you deal out to others, it will be dealt to you in return."

The Bible

9

Service
Pillar Three

Third pillar of "Chardi-kla" is Service. And, according to my research, service is the core of the Sikh way of living. Service for humanity dwells in the hearts of people, who practice "Chardi-kla".

With that, Sam drew the third pillar on the board.

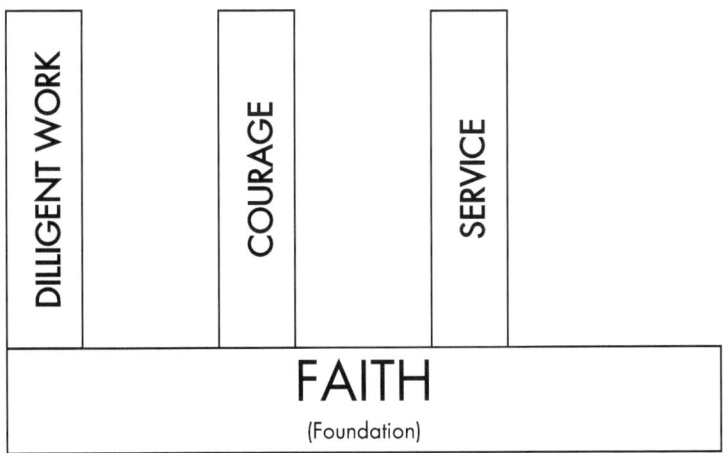

"According to these people, we are all born to serve each other, and that's what we are supposed to live by. The seed of service was planted into the Sikh faith on its origin."

"What do you mean by that? We all serve each other." asked Luis.

"I agree; humans depend on each other, and we try to serve each other; however, what I noticed is that these people have made service a part of their everyday life." replied Sam. They are so serious about unconditional service that they have made service part of their religious practice, and they call it Sewa.

"What do you mean by that?" asked Cynthia.

Sam answered that when you go to their temple (Guruduara), you will see people serving food in the communal kitchen. He said that he has even seen people clean and polish shoes in the shoe storage room at their temple.

"That's good, but what does that have to do with their financial success?" asked Cynthia.

"Everything." answered Sam. Their attitude about unconditional service doesn't just stay in the Temple, it stays with them all the time.

Studies show that people, who adopt the attitude of unconditional service, succeed in employment, business or any other field of life.

What I learned during my research is that, unconditional service is also linked to our spiritual lives. When we try to serve others, we are in tune with the nature of the Universe.

The Universal Power tries to serve the creation through people who provide unconditional service to the creation. Most people are willing to serve others, when they see the need. People tend to do dramatic acts to serve others in a big way, but that's not what service is all about, we can perform the smallest acts to serve others.

Shoe cleaning or polishing at the Sikh temple is a perfect example of a smallest act of service.

Like Mother Teresa said: 'We can do no great things, only small things with great love.'"

"But if we start serving others without charging them, how are we going to make a living?" asked Cynthia.

"I never said that you have to provide free service." replied Sam. People, who practice 'Chardi-kla', don't just focus on free service. It is a mindset. Whatever they do they consider it a service to humanity, and in return they get paid.

With the service mindset, we don't plan tactics to sell our products. We focus on finding ways to serve our fellow human beings, and in return, the Universe compensates us for our efforts.

Start to see everyone as a part of you. Provide honest service to solve their problems. When we provide unconditional service, we also get a feeling of satisfaction and a peace of mind, which is priceless.

When you practice 'Chardi-kla', you don't have any competition; what you have is an attitude of service. Serving others with compassion is so gratifying that you cannot be stopped.

God doesn't show up in person to answer our prayers. Our prayers are answered through the people who provide unconditional service.

The Punjabi people understand that we are the answers to other people's prayers, and they are compensated for their service and efforts.

"I also noticed that they are a close knit community." said Jason.

Sam said that it is true that they are a close knit community. They understand that the community needs are more important than the needs of individuals.

They are not just close to the Punjabi community. They promote close relations with everyone who comes into contact with them. They believe that as humans we should be concerned about everyone, and that is why during their daily prayers, they pray for everyone's good.

They pray: Sarbat da bhala (May good come to all).

"I have never heard that before! I guess, I didn't know that they are good people in the heart. I feel guilty now, because I have judged them by their looks, in the past. They deserve what they have. May god bless them" said Cynthia.

"Don't judge them by their looks. If you want to judge, then judge them by their achievements" said Sam.

"As I said before, you can practice the formula without following their faith." said Sam. Think about this third pillar, and provide unconditional service to humanity.

When we provide unconditional service to fellow human beings, we see the world from the Creator's point of view. We were provided with all the good things without being asked for anything in return.

The success of our life is not measured by the goods we own. It is measured by the service, we provide to others. We are here to serve our fellow human beings. So, adopt the service mindset.

Now, I will move onto the fourth pillar.

"Gratitude is not only the greatest of virtues, but the parent of all the other."

Anonymous

10

Gratitude
Pillar Four

The fourth pillar of Chardi-kla is Gratitude. It is a feeling of thankfulness for all that we have, in our lives. When our minds are filled with gratitude, we become an optimism machine.

Sam drew the fourth pillar on the board.

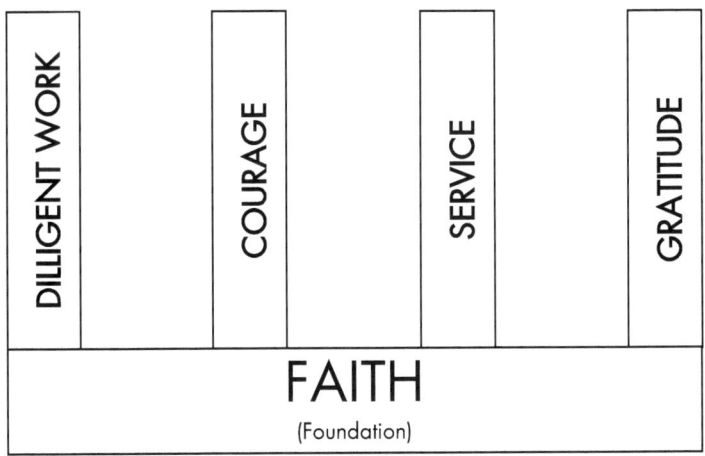

During my research, I found that the people who practice 'Chardi-kla' are optimism machines. When we practice gratitude, we develop an internal environment where we see the good in every situation. A life with the force of gratitude can survive anything.

"How can people be thankful, when they are facing adversities?" said Cynthia.

Sam said that adversities are a part of life. They make us stronger, if we learn from them. Unfortunately, some people believe that adversities are only for unlucky people.

We all face adversities. The sun goes down on all of us every day. When we practice gratitude, whatever comes our way, we consider it to be a gift from God.

Gratitude requires us to swallow our pride, and give the credit to others or God for whatever we receive. 'Chardi-kla' practitioners are masters at giving credit to God.

I read in a book during my research, that even Albert Einstein had to remind himself hundreds of times a day that his inner and outer life depends on other people.

"So, these people still thank God for all they have been through?" said Cynthia.

Yes, that's the magic of 'Chardi-kla'. They are trained from birth to be thankful. Actually, if you think about, it seems like all of the adversities they faced in the past (and still are facing) have made them stronger. They don't look at anything in terms of a problem. They look at the infinite possibilities of the future with a mindset of gratitude and keep moving forward.

Those who practice true gratitude feel that they have been called to do what they are doing. The Sikh people believe that the Creator has given duties to everyone, and that we perform according to God's will.

When we practice gratitude, we tend to give up excuses. As you may know excuses have been a part of human conditioning for a very long time.

With gratitude, we start to feel happy and develop flamboyancy in our personalities. We start to live excuse free life.

When times are tough, gratitude becomes even more important because it acts like a fireplace on a cold night. A feeling of gratitude gives us relief and hope. We keep pushing forward without seeing obstacles as being permanent.

We tend to forgive others and free ourselves from bitterness. We start to understand that God didn't make us any more special than other people. We start to appreciate all people this way.

Positive psychology studies show that gratitude is one of the few things, which can change lives. Studies also found that people who practice gratitude are happier and more pleasant to be around.

We develop this attitude by recognizing that we could not be where we are without the contribution of others. Jasvir set me straight by saying that we depend on others, even for eating.

This feeling of gratitude and gratefulness fills our heart with grace. We become humble and in tune with nature. We feel higher levels of positive emotions.

"We celebrate thanksgiving to express our gratitude..." said Cynthia.

"That is a very good tradition" said Sam". However, when you practice Chardikla, gratitude becomes part of your everyday life. It opens the doors for prosperity in your life.

We have to make a conscious decision to see our blessings, instead of curses. We need to accept our circumstances as they are.

If we cannot change our circumstances, we should learn to be grateful for them, because that's all we have, to work with. If we curse, what do we have to work with? What else is there?

When we adopt the attitude of gratitude, we learn to accept our circumstances, as they are, and try our best to deal with them. We consider them gifts from God.

What I learned, during my research is that with gratitude, our capacity for joy and happiness increases. This is very apparent in the personalities of the Punjabi people.

When we feel grateful, we tend to remember the beautiful things in life. Our focus changes from cursing, to appreciating the gifts of life. Gratefulness and a caring attitude becomes a part of us.

"So, people who practice this formula, become prosperous because they are thankful for what they have." said Cynthia.

"That is true" said Sam.

We have now covered all of the four pillars of 'Chardi-kla'. It will take a few more minutes to share with you the complete formula.

"I suggest that we take a break." said Luis.

Everyone agreed and class dispersed for a 10 minutes break.

"The mind is everything. What you think you become."

Buddha

11

Chardi-kla

As I said earlier, name of the success secret is – 'Chardi-kla'. And it is pronounced as:

Ch   as in <u>ch</u>apter
Ar   as in <u>are</u>
Di   as in <u>Dee</u>
Kla as in <u>Kla</u>us

It means: 'rising power of the mind'. It is an expression used for a focused and a high energy mind.

When we have the 'Chardi-kla' mindset, our mind is in continuous evolving state. We initiate extraordinary power within us, which can help us attain anything in life.

Sam drew a triangle on top of the pillars:

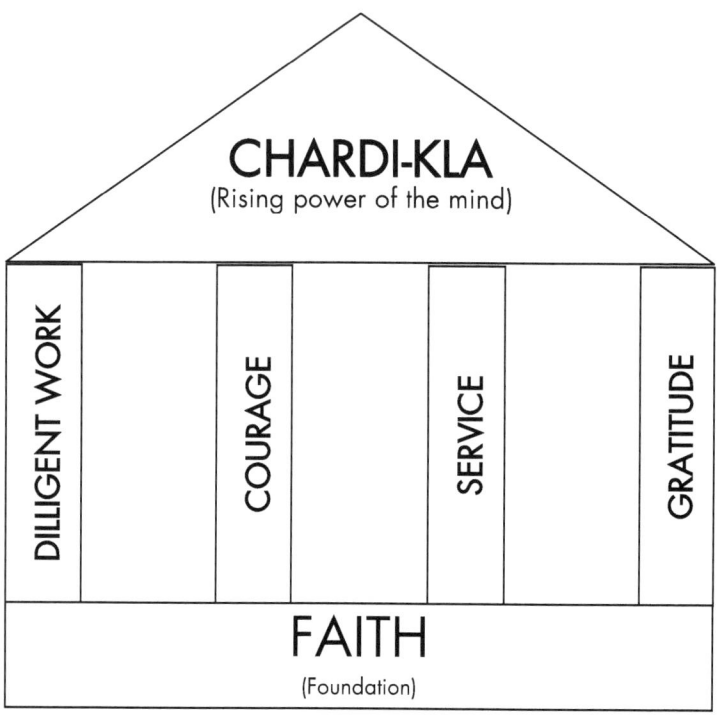

As you can see, 'Chardi-kla' is supported by four strong pillars, and a foundation of faith. It looks like a house, and we should let our mind live in this house, instead of letting it wander aimlessly.

As we protect our homes from invaders, so we should protect our mind. We let other people and negative circumstances invade our minds, and if our mind is invaded, our life becomes unpleasant.

People who practice 'Chardi-kla' decide who and what enters their mind. They protect it like a gold mine, because that is what it is.

When we practice 'Chardi-kla' our mind will manufacture elite thoughts and **our thoughts form our belief system**. It has been scientifically proven that **our belief system shapes our lives**.

Chardi-kla supports the belief that we are born to win. We attain the highest level of confidence and become winners.

With 'Chardi-kla", we also realize the true nature, because we are in tune with nature.

Alex explained that he read a book named "The Biology of Belief" written by cell biologist Bruce Lipton, Ph.D. In his book Dr. Lipton explains that our lives are controlled by our beliefs and the environment, and not by our genetic inheritance.

He states that genetically we receive a blue print as our DNA, and beliefs are the material, we use to shape our lives. According to Mr. Lipton, our beliefs can override our DNA.

"If that is true, then Chardi-kla would be a perfect belief system to have" said Luis. "It contains all the components of good living, including spirituality."

"I agree" said Sam. "Science is proving it now, but these guys have been using this consistently for more than 500 years."

Let me ask you a question now... Do you see any reason, why someone would fail in life, if they use this formula?

"I can't really think of any reason, at this moment;" said Bob. However, it depends on how effectively a person can use this formula."

"It's not hard at all. I have been practicing it for a while" said Sam "and the beauty of this is that it does not require us to practice the Sikh faith. There are no prayers, which we have to say in Punjabi. Another, fascinating fact, I found about these people is that their prayer starts with talking about a win.

"What?!" shouted Cynthia again.

"That's what I said, when I heard this!" said Sam. Their prayer starts like this: 'God is one; his name is true and victory belongs to God.' As I said earlier, they believe God is always with them. And, if the victorious God is with someone, why would they not feel victorious?"

"I guess that is true. No one is going to defeat God." said Luis.

You see, it is a state of mind, and a person has to practice and acquire it. It is a state of optimistic, high spirit, resilient and continuously evolving mind.

"Chardi-kla" allows one to sail through the adversities of life without much harm. A person, who is in the Chardi-kla state of mind, never accepts defeat.

We have already discussed that there are five components of this formula:

1. Faith (Foundation)
2. Work Diligently (Pillar 1)
3. Courage (Pillar 2)
4. Service (Pillar 3)
5. Gratitude (Pillar 4)

"I have studied a lot about the popular positive thinking models available today; I also tried practicing some of them as well. I even tried visualization techniques, but haven't had much success." said Alex, who has been sitting quietly in the corner.

"I have read in many books that visualization really works. Some people say that, they have achieved major successes" said Jason.

"I am sure some people have achieved success with visualization techniques." replied Sam. But, I have never tried it. By the way, how does visualization work?

Alex explained that there are many techniques, but basically you close your eyes and see your future the way you want it. The more you visualize, the better it gets. The clearer you can visualize the future, sooner it becomes your reality. Visualization makes that reality a part of you, and then that reality shows up in your life.

"So, you don't really do any actual work?" asked Sam.

"You do the work as well... and once your future becomes your reality you automatically start doing the work." replied Alex.

"As I said earlier, Chardi-kla has been in use for more than 500 years. And, as far as I know, no visualization is required to practice this formula." said Sam. I am not even sure, if people have the time to visualize their future. What I found in my life experience is that there is no substitute for hard work.

"There is one. Winning the lottery!" said Cynthia. Everyone had a good laugh at Cynthia's comment.

Sam said that winning the lottery might fix your financial problems, but it will create some new ones. Most people who win lotteries, end up destroying their lives, because they are not mentally prepared for money.

I can assure you that if you can learn how to practice 'Chardi-kla', you will fix your financial and other problems. You will learn to face your problems head on.

It is not a cumbersome formula. It is a way of life, and once you start using it; success will follow.

Now, I will talk about practicing 'Chardi-kla' effectively.

"Practice is the best of all instructors"
Publilius Syrus

12

Chardi-kla Practice

Scholars of the world have been trying to find out, why some people succeed and some fail. They have identified behavior patterns of successful people.

During my research, I have also identified the success secret of the Punjabi people. This success method is honed over many years, and it is delivering results.

"I'm sure every Punjabi is not that successful." said Luis.

"I agree." answered Sam. "There are a lot of Punjabi folks, which are just living average or below average lives. However, what I noticed is that most of them are living prosperous, happy and healthy lives.

I have already shared some statistics with you earlier, about their contribution. I am an immigrant into this Country, and what I noticed is that 30-40 percent of them are living an above average lifestyle, and others are living an average lifestyle.

I also noticed that the people, who are just living average lives, don't practice Chardi-kla diligently. They are living just average lives, because they don't nurture the seed of Chardi-kla that has been planted in them.

We all know what happens to seeds and plants when we don't nurture them. I hope that they all start practicing this formula diligently.

"May be some of them don't understand how valuable is this success secret" said Bob. "Science is proving today that wherever our mind goes, life goes."

"If they all start practicing this success formula, sky would be the limit for them!" said Cynthia.

"I agree" replied Sam. "if these people can really put this formula to work, they would be able to become more prosperous. Unfortunately, sometimes we don't realize what we have. Humans have a tendency to look for solutions outside. I noticed, during my research, that even some Punjabi's are doing the same."

"But if they don't want to practice, it's their choice. I suggest that you try practicing this in your life. You will definitely benefit from 'Chardi-kla', as I have."

"Now I would like to thank everyone for giving me the opportunity to share my research and this success secret. Try your best to stay in "Chardi-kla", and you will definitely become successful, as many have.

"If you ever have any questions about this, contact me, and I will get you the answer."

Everyone applauded Sam and he took the seat.

Luis got up and thanked Sam, for sharing this proven success secret with everyone. She encouraged everyone to practice and teach "Chardi-kla" and become successful.

She ended with saying "We are born to win, so let's use this formula and become winners!"

Chardi-kla Tips

Let's look at some basic tips, how to practice this formula.

- Write "Chardi-kla" on sticky notes and put the notes on your washroom mirror, your car steering wheel, your personal & office computers, and other visible places. The idea is to keep your mind focused on the formula. Remember, wherever our attention goes, life goes.
- Always remember that God is with you. Have complete faith in the Universal God.
- Think in terms of contributing to the society. We all know that "we reap what we sow" so plant the seeds of your contribution.
- Work diligently, because the harder we work, luckier we get.
- Be courageous and fearless. Remember God is fearless and He resides inside

you. Consider adversities to be your teachers.

- Think in terms of unconditional service to your fellow human beings. "Manas ki jaat sabhai akai pehchanbau" (Guru Granth Sahib) it means "Recognize the entire human race as one."

- Practice Gratitude in every moment. Always give credit to others for everything you have, because we depend on others for living.

- Try to associate with people who practice "Chardi-kla". It is contagious, and you will catch it. It will make it easier for you to adopt this success formula.

Benefits of Chardi-kla

Now, let's talk about some of the benefits of using this proven success formula:

- You will attain a peace of mind, which is the main goal of every human being.
- You will obtain higher levels of health. Medical community has proven that stress is the main cause of all the major diseases and when you are in the "Chardi-kla" state of mind, stress is nowhere to be found.
- You will attain better relations with everyone you come in contact with.
- You will gain financial prosperity.
- You will become a happier and a more flamboyant person that others will like and with whom they will want to spend time.
- You will have control over your life, because you will have control of your

mind. "Chardi-kla" and negative beliefs cannot live together in one mind.

- You will be able to manufacture your own future. You will expect the best, because expectations come from beliefs.
- You will become the winner in every life situation. And, that feeling of being a winner is priceless.
- You will start to like yourself. Because you are the best work of God, and He doesn't make junk.

A Note for Managers

Last but not least a quick note for business owners, managers and leaders.

Would you want to have an employee, who is extremely skilled or an employee who has a winner's attitude?

People with a winner's attitude are hard to find. Skills can be taught, whereas attitude is an individual matter.

Experienced managers understand that employees with bad attitudes can reduce the effectiveness and productivity of the whole organization.

Finding one person who understands "Chardi-kla" and practices it diligently will create a better team. Better yet, find a person who's DNA includes 'Chardi-kla' and this person will act as a catalyst to enhance your team. He will improve the behavior of coworkers, and you will reap the benefits of effective, pleasant and driven workforce.

"Get together, my brethren, and remove all misunderstandings through regard for each other"
Guru Granth Sahib

About the Author

PJ is a financial advisor in Calgary (Canada). He provides multiple financial planning services, including; Life insurances, Mortgage insurances, Mortgages, Tax services, etc.

He is also a personal development mentor, and is very passionate about helping others succeed. He practices "Chardi-kla" religiously, and has been helping people to do the same.

He speaks on multiple personal development topics. He believes in taking continuous actions towards specific goals with measured progress. Furthermore, he believes that "Chardi-kla" is the best formula to live happy, healthy and prosperous life.

He issues a bi-weekly success basics newsletter. You can subscribe to the newsletter at: **www.success-basics.com.**

PJ has a weekly personal development radio talk show (Wednesday at 6:00pm, Mountain Time) on radio "Sursangam" in Calgary. His program can be listened on the internet on http://www.radiosursangam.com.

6415938R0

Made in the USA
Charleston, SC
22 October 2010